Stock Trading
Notebook

TRADES...WATCHLISTS...CONTACTS...NOTES...FOR...STOCK...INVESTORS

THIS LOG BOOK BELONGS TO

Buckets

Designed by SkullPilot Publishing
Copyright © SkullPilot Publishing (2019)

All rights reserved. No part of this publication may be reproduced, stored in a retrieval system, or transmitted in any form, including photocopying, electronic, mechanical or recording, without the written consent of the author.

Cover images reproduced with permission under the Creative Commons Attribution Generic Licence, and/or under Creative Commons Zero (Public Domain) Licence.

Important Contacts

Name	Number/Email	Name	Number/Email

Glossary

Market Capitalization
Current share price multiplied by total number of shares.

P/E Ratio
A stock's price divided by its earnings per share. Indicates whether market is under- or over-valuing the company.

EV/EBITDA
Enterprise Value=Market Cap plus Debt minus Cash. Gives better company valuation than P/E as it takes debt into account.

Debt-to-Equity Ratio
Indicates how much debt is involved in the business versus shareholder equity (ie how leveraged).

Return on Equity (ROE)
Good indicator of capability of company management. ROE=Net Income divided by Shareholder Equity.

Current Ratio
Indicator of liquidity - can company meet short-term obligations. Current ratio= Current Assets divided by Current Liabilities.

Dividend Yield
Dividend per share divided by the share price.

Earnings per Share
Net earnings of the company divided by the number of shares.

Notes

Notes

Notes

Notes

Stock Name	Code	Qty	Date	Buy Price	Date	Sell Price

Notes

Target Price	Stop Price	Total Cost	Net Return	Profit (Loss)	Notes/Comments

Notes

Stock Name	Code	Qty	Date	Buy Price	Date	Sell Price

Notes

Target Price	Stop Price	Total Cost	Net Return	Profit (Loss)	Notes/Comments

Notes

Stock Name	Code	Qty	Date	Buy Price	Date	Sell Price

Notes

Target Price	Stop Price	Total Cost	Net Return	Profit (Loss)	Notes/Comments

Notes

Stock Name	Code	Qty	Date	Buy Price	Date	Sell Price

Notes

Target Price	Stop Price	Total Cost	Net Return	Profit (Loss)	Notes/Comments

Notes

Stock Name	Code	Qty	Date	Buy Price	Date	Sell Price

Notes

Target Price	Stop Price	Total Cost	Net Return	Profit (Loss)	Notes/Comments

Notes

Stock Name	Code	Qty	Date	Buy Price	Date	Sell Price

Notes

Target Price	Stop Price	Total Cost	Net Return	Profit (Loss)	Notes/Comments

Notes

Stock Name	Code	Qty	Date	Buy Price	Date	Sell Price

Notes

Target Price	Stop Price	Total Cost	Net Return	Profit (Loss)	Notes/Comments

Notes

Stock Name	Code	Qty	Date	Buy Price	Date	Sell Price

Notes

Target Price	Stop Price	Total Cost	Net Return	Profit (Loss)	Notes/Comments

Notes

Stock Name	Code	Qty	Date	Buy Price	Date	Sell Price

Notes

Target Price	Stop Price	Total Cost	Net Return	Profit (Loss)	Notes/Comments

Notes

Stock Name	Code	Qty	Date	Buy Price	Date	Sell Price

Notes

Target Price	Stop Price	Total Cost	Net Return	Profit (Loss)	Notes/Comments

Notes

Stock Name	Code	Qty	Date	Buy Price	Date	Sell Price

Notes

Target Price	Stop Price	Total Cost	Net Return	Profit (Loss)	Notes/Comments

Notes

Stock Name	Code	Qty	Date	Buy Price	Date	Sell Price

Notes

Target Price	Stop Price	Total Cost	Net Return	Profit (Loss)	Notes/Comments

Notes

Stock Name	Code	Qty	Date	Buy Price	Date	Sell Price

Notes

Target Price	Stop Price	Total Cost	Net Return	Profit (Loss)	Notes/Comments

Notes

Stock Name	Code	Qty	Date	Buy Price	Date	Sell Price

Notes

Target Price	Stop Price	Total Cost	Net Return	Profit (Loss)	Notes/Comments

Notes

Stock Name	Code	Qty	Date	Buy Price	Date	Sell Price

Notes

Target Price	Stop Price	Total Cost	Net Return	Profit (Loss)	Notes/Comments

Notes

Stock Name	Code	Qty	Date	Buy Price	Date	Sell Price

Notes

Target Price	Stop Price	Total Cost	Net Return	Profit (Loss)	Notes/Comments

Notes

Stock Name	Code	Qty	Date	Buy Price	Date	Sell Price

Notes

Target Price	Stop Price	Total Cost	Net Return	Profit (Loss)	Notes/Comments

Notes

Stock Name	Code	Qty	Date	Buy Price	Date	Sell Price

Notes

Target Price	Stop Price	Total Cost	Net Return	Profit (Loss)	Notes/Comments

Notes

Stock Name	Code	Qty	Date	Buy Price	Date	Sell Price

Notes

Target Price	Stop Price	Total Cost	Net Return	Profit (Loss)	Notes/Comments

Notes

Stock Name	Code	Qty	Date	Buy Price	Date	Sell Price

Notes

Target Price	Stop Price	Total Cost	Net Return	Profit (Loss)	Notes/Comments

Notes

Stock Name	Code	Qty	Date	Buy Price	Date	Sell Price

Notes

Target Price	Stop Price	Total Cost	Net Return	Profit (Loss)	Notes/Comments

Notes

Stock Name	Code	Qty	Date	Buy Price	Date	Sell Price

Notes

Target Price	Stop Price	Total Cost	Net Return	Profit (Loss)	Notes/Comments

Notes

Stock Name	Code	Qty	Date	Buy Price	Date	Sell Price

Notes

Target Price	Stop Price	Total Cost	Net Return	Profit (Loss)	Notes/Comments

Notes

Stock Name	Code	Qty	Date	Buy Price	Date	Sell Price

Notes

Target Price	Stop Price	Total Cost	Net Return	Profit (Loss)	Notes/Comments

Notes

Stock Name	Code	Qty	Date	Buy Price	Date	Sell Price

Notes

Target Price	Stop Price	Total Cost	Net Return	Profit (Loss)	Notes/Comments

Notes

Stock Name	Code	Qty	Date	Buy Price	Date	Sell Price

Notes

Target Price	Stop Price	Total Cost	Net Return	Profit (Loss)	Notes/Comments

Notes

Stock Name	Code	Qty	Date	Buy Price	Date	Sell Price

Notes

Target Price	Stop Price	Total Cost	Net Return	Profit (Loss)	Notes/Comments

Notes

Stock Name	Code	Qty	Date	Buy Price	Date	Sell Price

Notes

Target Price	Stop Price	Total Cost	Net Return	Profit (Loss)	Notes/Comments

Notes

Stock Name	Code	Qty	Date	Buy Price	Date	Sell Price

Notes

Target Price	Stop Price	Total Cost	Net Return	Profit (Loss)	Notes/Comments

Notes

Stock Name	Code	Qty	Date	Buy Price	Date	Sell Price

Notes

Target Price	Stop Price	Total Cost	Net Return	Profit (Loss)	Notes/Comments

Notes

Stock Name	Code	Qty	Date	Buy Price	Date	Sell Price

Notes

Target Price	Stop Price	Total Cost	Net Return	Profit (Loss)	Notes/Comments

Notes

Stock Name	Code	Qty	Date	Buy Price	Date	Sell Price

Notes

Target Price	Stop Price	Total Cost	Net Return	Profit (Loss)	Notes/Comments

Notes

Stock Name	Code	Qty	Date	Buy Price	Date	Sell Price

Notes

Target Price	Stop Price	Total Cost	Net Return	Profit (Loss)	Notes/Comments

Notes

Stock Name	Code	Qty	Date	Buy Price	Date	Sell Price

Notes

Target Price	Stop Price	Total Cost	Net Return	Profit (Loss)	Notes/Comments

Notes

Stock Name	Code	Qty	Date	Buy Price	Date	Sell Price

Notes

Target Price	Stop Price	Total Cost	Net Return	Profit (Loss)	Notes/Comments

Notes

Stock Name	Code	Qty	Date	Buy Price	Date	Sell Price

Notes

Target Price	Stop Price	Total Cost	Net Return	Profit (Loss)	Notes/Comments

Notes

Stock Buying Watchlist

Company			Code	Sector		Index	Market Cap
P/E Ratio	EV/EBITDA	Debt-to-Equity	ROE	Current Ratio		Dividend Yield	Earnings per Share
Research Notes						Date	Price

Company			Code	Sector		Index	Market Cap
P/E Ratio	EV/EBITDA	Debt-to-Equity	ROE	Current Ratio		Dividend Yield	Earnings per Share
Research Notes						Date	Price

Company			Code	Sector		Index	Market Cap
P/E Ratio	EV/EBITDA	Debt-to-Equity	ROE	Current Ratio		Dividend Yield	Earnings per Share
Research Notes						Date	Price

Company			Code	Sector		Index	Market Cap
P/E Ratio	EV/EBITDA	Debt-to-Equity	ROE	Current Ratio		Dividend Yield	Earnings per Share
Research Notes						Date	Price

Stock Buying Watchlist

Company			Code	Sector	Index	Market Cap
P/E Ratio	EV/EBITDA	Debt-to-Equity	ROE	Current Ratio	Dividend Yield	Earnings per Share
Research Notes					Date	Price

Company			Code	Sector	Index	Market Cap
P/E Ratio	EV/EBITDA	Debt-to-Equity	ROE	Current Ratio	Dividend Yield	Earnings per Share
Research Notes					Date	Price

Company			Code	Sector	Index	Market Cap
P/E Ratio	EV/EBITDA	Debt-to-Equity	ROE	Current Ratio	Dividend Yield	Earnings per Share
Research Notes					Date	Price

Company			Code	Sector	Index	Market Cap
P/E Ratio	EV/EBITDA	Debt-to-Equity	ROE	Current Ratio	Dividend Yield	Earnings per Share
Research Notes					Date	Price

Stock Buying Watchlist

Company			Code	Sector	Index	Market Cap
P/E Ratio	EV/EBITDA	Debt-to-Equity	ROE	Current Ratio	Dividend Yield	Earnings per Share
Research Notes					Date	Price

Company			Code	Sector	Index	Market Cap
P/E Ratio	EV/EBITDA	Debt-to-Equity	ROE	Current Ratio	Dividend Yield	Earnings per Share
Research Notes					Date	Price

Company			Code	Sector	Index	Market Cap
P/E Ratio	EV/EBITDA	Debt-to-Equity	ROE	Current Ratio	Dividend Yield	Earnings per Share
Research Notes					Date	Price

Company			Code	Sector	Index	Market Cap
P/E Ratio	EV/EBITDA	Debt-to-Equity	ROE	Current Ratio	Dividend Yield	Earnings per Share
Research Notes					Date	Price

Stock Buying Watchlist

Company			Code	Sector	Index	Market Cap
P/E Ratio	EV/EBITDA	Debt-to-Equity	ROE	Current Ratio	Dividend Yield	Earnings per Share
Research Notes					Date	Price

Company			Code	Sector	Index	Market Cap
P/E Ratio	EV/EBITDA	Debt-to-Equity	ROE	Current Ratio	Dividend Yield	Earnings per Share
Research Notes					Date	Price

Company			Code	Sector	Index	Market Cap
P/E Ratio	EV/EBITDA	Debt-to-Equity	ROE	Current Ratio	Dividend Yield	Earnings per Share
Research Notes					Date	Price

Company			Code	Sector	Index	Market Cap
P/E Ratio	EV/EBITDA	Debt-to-Equity	ROE	Current Ratio	Dividend Yield	Earnings per Share
Research Notes					Date	Price

Stock Buying Watchlist

Company			Code	Sector	Index	Market Cap
P/E Ratio	EV/EBITDA	Debt-to-Equity	ROE	Current Ratio	Dividend Yield	Earnings per Share
Research Notes					Date	Price

Company			Code	Sector	Index	Market Cap
P/E Ratio	EV/EBITDA	Debt-to-Equity	ROE	Current Ratio	Dividend Yield	Earnings per Share
Research Notes					Date	Price

Company			Code	Sector	Index	Market Cap
P/E Ratio	EV/EBITDA	Debt-to-Equity	ROE	Current Ratio	Dividend Yield	Earnings per Share
Research Notes					Date	Price

Company			Code	Sector	Index	Market Cap
P/E Ratio	EV/EBITDA	Debt-to-Equity	ROE	Current Ratio	Dividend Yield	Earnings per Share
Research Notes					Date	Price

Stock Buying Watchlist

Company				Code	Sector	Index	Market Cap
P/E Ratio	EV/EBITDA	Debt-to-Equity	ROE		Current Ratio	Dividend Yield	Earnings per Share
Research Notes						Date	Price

Company				Code	Sector	Index	Market Cap
P/E Ratio	EV/EBITDA	Debt-to-Equity	ROE		Current Ratio	Dividend Yield	Earnings per Share
Research Notes						Date	Price

Company				Code	Sector	Index	Market Cap
P/E Ratio	EV/EBITDA	Debt-to-Equity	ROE		Current Ratio	Dividend Yield	Earnings per Share
Research Notes						Date	Price

Company				Code	Sector	Index	Market Cap
P/E Ratio	EV/EBITDA	Debt-to-Equity	ROE		Current Ratio	Dividend Yield	Earnings per Share
Research Notes						Date	Price

Stock Buying Watchlist

Company			Code	Sector	Index	Market Cap
P/E Ratio	EV/EBITDA	Debt-to-Equity	ROE	Current Ratio	Dividend Yield	Earnings per Share
Research Notes					Date	Price

Company			Code	Sector	Index	Market Cap
P/E Ratio	EV/EBITDA	Debt-to-Equity	ROE	Current Ratio	Dividend Yield	Earnings per Share
Research Notes					Date	Price

Company			Code	Sector	Index	Market Cap
P/E Ratio	EV/EBITDA	Debt-to-Equity	ROE	Current Ratio	Dividend Yield	Earnings per Share
Research Notes					Date	Price

Company			Code	Sector	Index	Market Cap
P/E Ratio	EV/EBITDA	Debt-to-Equity	ROE	Current Ratio	Dividend Yield	Earnings per Share
Research Notes					Date	Price

Stock Buying Watchlist

Company				Code	Sector	Index	Market Cap
P/E Ratio	EV/EBITDA	Debt-to-Equity		ROE	Current Ratio	Dividend Yield	Earnings per Share
Research Notes						Date	Price

Company				Code	Sector	Index	Market Cap
P/E Ratio	EV/EBITDA	Debt-to-Equity		ROE	Current Ratio	Dividend Yield	Earnings per Share
Research Notes						Date	Price

Company				Code	Sector	Index	Market Cap
P/E Ratio	EV/EBITDA	Debt-to-Equity		ROE	Current Ratio	Dividend Yield	Earnings per Share
Research Notes						Date	Price

Company				Code	Sector	Index	Market Cap
P/E Ratio	EV/EBITDA	Debt-to-Equity		ROE	Current Ratio	Dividend Yield	Earnings per Share
Research Notes						Date	Price

Stock Buying Watchlist

Company				Code	Sector		Index	Market Cap
P/E Ratio	EV/EBITDA	Debt-to-Equity		ROE	Current Ratio		Dividend Yield	Earnings per Share
Research Notes							Date	Price

Company				Code	Sector		Index	Market Cap
P/E Ratio	EV/EBITDA	Debt-to-Equity		ROE	Current Ratio		Dividend Yield	Earnings per Share
Research Notes							Date	Price

Company				Code	Sector		Index	Market Cap
P/E Ratio	EV/EBITDA	Debt-to-Equity		ROE	Current Ratio		Dividend Yield	Earnings per Share
Research Notes							Date	Price

Company				Code	Sector		Index	Market Cap
P/E Ratio	EV/EBITDA	Debt-to-Equity		ROE	Current Ratio		Dividend Yield	Earnings per Share
Research Notes							Date	Price

Stock Buying Watchlist

Company				Code	Sector	Index	Market Cap
P/E Ratio	EV/EBITDA	Debt-to-Equity		ROE	Current Ratio	Dividend Yield	Earnings per Share
Research Notes						Date	Price

Company				Code	Sector	Index	Market Cap
P/E Ratio	EV/EBITDA	Debt-to-Equity		ROE	Current Ratio	Dividend Yield	Earnings per Share
Research Notes						Date	Price

Company				Code	Sector	Index	Market Cap
P/E Ratio	EV/EBITDA	Debt-to-Equity		ROE	Current Ratio	Dividend Yield	Earnings per Share
Research Notes						Date	Price

Company				Code	Sector	Index	Market Cap
P/E Ratio	EV/EBITDA	Debt-to-Equity		ROE	Current Ratio	Dividend Yield	Earnings per Share
Research Notes						Date	Price

Stock Buying Watchlist

Company				Code	Sector	Index	Market Cap
P/E Ratio	EV/EBITDA	Debt-to-Equity	ROE		Current Ratio	Dividend Yield	Earnings per Share
Research Notes						Date	Price

Company				Code	Sector	Index	Market Cap
P/E Ratio	EV/EBITDA	Debt-to-Equity	ROE		Current Ratio	Dividend Yield	Earnings per Share
Research Notes						Date	Price

Company				Code	Sector	Index	Market Cap
P/E Ratio	EV/EBITDA	Debt-to-Equity	ROE		Current Ratio	Dividend Yield	Earnings per Share
Research Notes						Date	Price

Company				Code	Sector	Index	Market Cap
P/E Ratio	EV/EBITDA	Debt-to-Equity	ROE		Current Ratio	Dividend Yield	Earnings per Share
Research Notes						Date	Price

Stock Buying Watchlist

Company			Code	Sector	Index	Market Cap
P/E Ratio	EV/EBITDA	Debt-to-Equity	ROE	Current Ratio	Dividend Yield	Earnings per Share
Research Notes					Date	Price

Company			Code	Sector	Index	Market Cap
P/E Ratio	EV/EBITDA	Debt-to-Equity	ROE	Current Ratio	Dividend Yield	Earnings per Share
Research Notes					Date	Price

Company			Code	Sector	Index	Market Cap
P/E Ratio	EV/EBITDA	Debt-to-Equity	ROE	Current Ratio	Dividend Yield	Earnings per Share
Research Notes					Date	Price

Company			Code	Sector	Index	Market Cap
P/E Ratio	EV/EBITDA	Debt-to-Equity	ROE	Current Ratio	Dividend Yield	Earnings per Share
Research Notes					Date	Price

Stock Buying Watchlist

Company				Code	Sector		Index	Market Cap
P/E Ratio	EV/EBITDA	Debt-to-Equity		ROE	Current Ratio		Dividend Yield	Earnings per Share
Research Notes							Date	Price

Company				Code	Sector		Index	Market Cap
P/E Ratio	EV/EBITDA	Debt-to-Equity		ROE	Current Ratio		Dividend Yield	Earnings per Share
Research Notes							Date	Price

Company				Code	Sector		Index	Market Cap
P/E Ratio	EV/EBITDA	Debt-to-Equity		ROE	Current Ratio		Dividend Yield	Earnings per Share
Research Notes							Date	Price

Company				Code	Sector		Index	Market Cap
P/E Ratio	EV/EBITDA	Debt-to-Equity		ROE	Current Ratio		Dividend Yield	Earnings per Share
Research Notes							Date	Price

Stock Buying Watchlist

Company				Code	Sector		Index	Market Cap
P/E Ratio	EV/EBITDA	Debt-to-Equity		ROE	Current Ratio		Dividend Yield	Earnings per Share
Research Notes							Date	Price

Company				Code	Sector		Index	Market Cap
P/E Ratio	EV/EBITDA	Debt-to-Equity		ROE	Current Ratio		Dividend Yield	Earnings per Share
Research Notes							Date	Price

Company				Code	Sector		Index	Market Cap
P/E Ratio	EV/EBITDA	Debt-to-Equity		ROE	Current Ratio		Dividend Yield	Earnings per Share
Research Notes							Date	Price

Company				Code	Sector		Index	Market Cap
P/E Ratio	EV/EBITDA	Debt-to-Equity		ROE	Current Ratio		Dividend Yield	Earnings per Share
Research Notes							Date	Price

Stock Buying Watchlist

Company				Code	Sector	Index	Market Cap
P/E Ratio	EV/EBITDA	Debt-to-Equity		ROE	Current Ratio	Dividend Yield	Earnings per Share
Research Notes						Date	Price

Company				Code	Sector	Index	Market Cap
P/E Ratio	EV/EBITDA	Debt-to-Equity		ROE	Current Ratio	Dividend Yield	Earnings per Share
Research Notes						Date	Price

Company				Code	Sector	Index	Market Cap
P/E Ratio	EV/EBITDA	Debt-to-Equity		ROE	Current Ratio	Dividend Yield	Earnings per Share
Research Notes						Date	Price

Company				Code	Sector	Index	Market Cap
P/E Ratio	EV/EBITDA	Debt-to-Equity		ROE	Current Ratio	Dividend Yield	Earnings per Share
Research Notes						Date	Price

Stock Buying Watchlist

Company				Code	Sector	Index	Market Cap
P/E Ratio	EV/EBITDA	Debt-to-Equity		ROE	Current Ratio	Dividend Yield	Earnings per Share
Research Notes						Date	Price

Company				Code	Sector	Index	Market Cap
P/E Ratio	EV/EBITDA	Debt-to-Equity		ROE	Current Ratio	Dividend Yield	Earnings per Share
Research Notes						Date	Price

Company				Code	Sector	Index	Market Cap
P/E Ratio	EV/EBITDA	Debt-to-Equity		ROE	Current Ratio	Dividend Yield	Earnings per Share
Research Notes						Date	Price

Company				Code	Sector	Index	Market Cap
P/E Ratio	EV/EBITDA	Debt-to-Equity		ROE	Current Ratio	Dividend Yield	Earnings per Share
Research Notes						Date	Price

Stock Buying Watchlist

Company				Code	Sector	Index	Market Cap
P/E Ratio	EV/EBITDA	Debt-to-Equity	ROE		Current Ratio	Dividend Yield	Earnings per Share
Research Notes						Date	Price

Company				Code	Sector	Index	Market Cap
P/E Ratio	EV/EBITDA	Debt-to-Equity	ROE		Current Ratio	Dividend Yield	Earnings per Share
Research Notes						Date	Price

Company				Code	Sector	Index	Market Cap
P/E Ratio	EV/EBITDA	Debt-to-Equity	ROE		Current Ratio	Dividend Yield	Earnings per Share
Research Notes						Date	Price

Company				Code	Sector	Index	Market Cap
P/E Ratio	EV/EBITDA	Debt-to-Equity	ROE		Current Ratio	Dividend Yield	Earnings per Share
Research Notes						Date	Price

Stock Buying Watchlist

Company			Code	Sector	Index	Market Cap
P/E Ratio	EV/EBITDA	Debt-to-Equity	ROE	Current Ratio	Dividend Yield	Earnings per Share
Research Notes					Date	Price

Company			Code	Sector	Index	Market Cap
P/E Ratio	EV/EBITDA	Debt-to-Equity	ROE	Current Ratio	Dividend Yield	Earnings per Share
Research Notes					Date	Price

Company			Code	Sector	Index	Market Cap
P/E Ratio	EV/EBITDA	Debt-to-Equity	ROE	Current Ratio	Dividend Yield	Earnings per Share
Research Notes					Date	Price

Company			Code	Sector	Index	Market Cap
P/E Ratio	EV/EBITDA	Debt-to-Equity	ROE	Current Ratio	Dividend Yield	Earnings per Share
Research Notes					Date	Price

Stock Buying Watchlist

Company				Code	Sector		Index	Market Cap
P/E Ratio	EV/EBITDA	Debt-to-Equity		ROE	Current Ratio		Dividend Yield	Earnings per Share
Research Notes							Date	Price

Company				Code	Sector		Index	Market Cap
P/E Ratio	EV/EBITDA	Debt-to-Equity		ROE	Current Ratio		Dividend Yield	Earnings per Share
Research Notes							Date	Price

Company				Code	Sector		Index	Market Cap
P/E Ratio	EV/EBITDA	Debt-to-Equity		ROE	Current Ratio		Dividend Yield	Earnings per Share
Research Notes							Date	Price

Company				Code	Sector		Index	Market Cap
P/E Ratio	EV/EBITDA	Debt-to-Equity		ROE	Current Ratio		Dividend Yield	Earnings per Share
Research Notes							Date	Price

Stock Buying Watchlist

Company			Code	Sector	Index	Market Cap
P/E Ratio	EV/EBITDA	Debt-to-Equity	ROE	Current Ratio	Dividend Yield	Earnings per Share
Research Notes					Date	Price

Company			Code	Sector	Index	Market Cap
P/E Ratio	EV/EBITDA	Debt-to-Equity	ROE	Current Ratio	Dividend Yield	Earnings per Share
Research Notes					Date	Price

Company			Code	Sector	Index	Market Cap
P/E Ratio	EV/EBITDA	Debt-to-Equity	ROE	Current Ratio	Dividend Yield	Earnings per Share
Research Notes					Date	Price

Company			Code	Sector	Index	Market Cap
P/E Ratio	EV/EBITDA	Debt-to-Equity	ROE	Current Ratio	Dividend Yield	Earnings per Share
Research Notes					Date	Price

Stock Buying Watchlist

Company				Code	Sector		Index	Market Cap
P/E Ratio	EV/EBITDA	Debt-to-Equity		ROE	Current Ratio		Dividend Yield	Earnings per Share
Research Notes							Date	Price

Company				Code	Sector		Index	Market Cap
P/E Ratio	EV/EBITDA	Debt-to-Equity		ROE	Current Ratio		Dividend Yield	Earnings per Share
Research Notes							Date	Price

Company				Code	Sector		Index	Market Cap
P/E Ratio	EV/EBITDA	Debt-to-Equity		ROE	Current Ratio		Dividend Yield	Earnings per Share
Research Notes							Date	Price

Company				Code	Sector		Index	Market Cap
P/E Ratio	EV/EBITDA	Debt-to-Equity		ROE	Current Ratio		Dividend Yield	Earnings per Share
Research Notes							Date	Price

Stock Buying Watchlist

Company			Code	Sector	Index	Market Cap
P/E Ratio	EV/EBITDA	Debt-to-Equity	ROE	Current Ratio	Dividend Yield	Earnings per Share
Research Notes					Date	Price

Company			Code	Sector	Index	Market Cap
P/E Ratio	EV/EBITDA	Debt-to-Equity	ROE	Current Ratio	Dividend Yield	Earnings per Share
Research Notes					Date	Price

Company			Code	Sector	Index	Market Cap
P/E Ratio	EV/EBITDA	Debt-to-Equity	ROE	Current Ratio	Dividend Yield	Earnings per Share
Research Notes					Date	Price

Company			Code	Sector	Index	Market Cap
P/E Ratio	EV/EBITDA	Debt-to-Equity	ROE	Current Ratio	Dividend Yield	Earnings per Share
Research Notes					Date	Price

Stock Buying Watchlist

Company				Code	Sector		Index	Market Cap
P/E Ratio	EV/EBITDA	Debt-to-Equity		ROE	Current Ratio		Dividend Yield	Earnings per Share
Research Notes							Date	Price

Company				Code	Sector		Index	Market Cap
P/E Ratio	EV/EBITDA	Debt-to-Equity		ROE	Current Ratio		Dividend Yield	Earnings per Share
Research Notes							Date	Price

Company				Code	Sector		Index	Market Cap
P/E Ratio	EV/EBITDA	Debt-to-Equity		ROE	Current Ratio		Dividend Yield	Earnings per Share
Research Notes							Date	Price

Company				Code	Sector		Index	Market Cap
P/E Ratio	EV/EBITDA	Debt-to-Equity		ROE	Current Ratio		Dividend Yield	Earnings per Share
Research Notes							Date	Price

Stock Buying Watchlist

Company				Code	Sector	Index	Market Cap
P/E Ratio	EV/EBITDA	Debt-to-Equity	ROE		Current Ratio	Dividend Yield	Earnings per Share
Research Notes						Date	Price

Company				Code	Sector	Index	Market Cap
P/E Ratio	EV/EBITDA	Debt-to-Equity	ROE		Current Ratio	Dividend Yield	Earnings per Share
Research Notes						Date	Price

Company				Code	Sector	Index	Market Cap
P/E Ratio	EV/EBITDA	Debt-to-Equity	ROE		Current Ratio	Dividend Yield	Earnings per Share
Research Notes						Date	Price

Company				Code	Sector	Index	Market Cap
P/E Ratio	EV/EBITDA	Debt-to-Equity	ROE		Current Ratio	Dividend Yield	Earnings per Share
Research Notes						Date	Price

Stock Buying Watchlist

Company			Code	Sector	Index	Market Cap
P/E Ratio	EV/EBITDA	Debt-to-Equity	ROE	Current Ratio	Dividend Yield	Earnings per Share
Research Notes					Date	Price

Company			Code	Sector	Index	Market Cap
P/E Ratio	EV/EBITDA	Debt-to-Equity	ROE	Current Ratio	Dividend Yield	Earnings per Share
Research Notes					Date	Price

Company			Code	Sector	Index	Market Cap
P/E Ratio	EV/EBITDA	Debt-to-Equity	ROE	Current Ratio	Dividend Yield	Earnings per Share
Research Notes					Date	Price

Company			Code	Sector	Index	Market Cap
P/E Ratio	EV/EBITDA	Debt-to-Equity	ROE	Current Ratio	Dividend Yield	Earnings per Share
Research Notes					Date	Price

Stock Buying Watchlist

Company			Code	Sector	Index	Market Cap
P/E Ratio	EV/EBITDA	Debt-to-Equity	ROE	Current Ratio	Dividend Yield	Earnings per Share
Research Notes					Date	Price

Company			Code	Sector	Index	Market Cap
P/E Ratio	EV/EBITDA	Debt-to-Equity	ROE	Current Ratio	Dividend Yield	Earnings per Share
Research Notes					Date	Price

Company			Code	Sector	Index	Market Cap
P/E Ratio	EV/EBITDA	Debt-to-Equity	ROE	Current Ratio	Dividend Yield	Earnings per Share
Research Notes					Date	Price

Company			Code	Sector	Index	Market Cap
P/E Ratio	EV/EBITDA	Debt-to-Equity	ROE	Current Ratio	Dividend Yield	Earnings per Share
Research Notes					Date	Price

Stock Buying Watchlist

Company			Code	Sector	Index	Market Cap
P/E Ratio	EV/EBITDA	Debt-to-Equity	ROE	Current Ratio	Dividend Yield	Earnings per Share
Research Notes					Date	Price

Company			Code	Sector	Index	Market Cap
P/E Ratio	EV/EBITDA	Debt-to-Equity	ROE	Current Ratio	Dividend Yield	Earnings per Share
Research Notes					Date	Price

Company			Code	Sector	Index	Market Cap
P/E Ratio	EV/EBITDA	Debt-to-Equity	ROE	Current Ratio	Dividend Yield	Earnings per Share
Research Notes					Date	Price

Company			Code	Sector	Index	Market Cap
P/E Ratio	EV/EBITDA	Debt-to-Equity	ROE	Current Ratio	Dividend Yield	Earnings per Share
Research Notes					Date	Price

Stock Buying Watchlist

Company			Code	Sector	Index	Market Cap
P/E Ratio	EV/EBITDA	Debt-to-Equity	ROE	Current Ratio	Dividend Yield	Earnings per Share
Research Notes					Date	Price

Company			Code	Sector	Index	Market Cap
P/E Ratio	EV/EBITDA	Debt-to-Equity	ROE	Current Ratio	Dividend Yield	Earnings per Share
Research Notes					Date	Price

Company			Code	Sector	Index	Market Cap
P/E Ratio	EV/EBITDA	Debt-to-Equity	ROE	Current Ratio	Dividend Yield	Earnings per Share
Research Notes					Date	Price

Company			Code	Sector	Index	Market Cap
P/E Ratio	EV/EBITDA	Debt-to-Equity	ROE	Current Ratio	Dividend Yield	Earnings per Share
Research Notes					Date	Price

Stock Buying Watchlist

Company			Code	Sector	Index	Market Cap
P/E Ratio	EV/EBITDA	Debt-to-Equity	ROE	Current Ratio	Dividend Yield	Earnings per Share
Research Notes					Date	Price

Company			Code	Sector	Index	Market Cap
P/E Ratio	EV/EBITDA	Debt-to-Equity	ROE	Current Ratio	Dividend Yield	Earnings per Share
Research Notes					Date	Price

Company			Code	Sector	Index	Market Cap
P/E Ratio	EV/EBITDA	Debt-to-Equity	ROE	Current Ratio	Dividend Yield	Earnings per Share
Research Notes					Date	Price

Company			Code	Sector	Index	Market Cap
P/E Ratio	EV/EBITDA	Debt-to-Equity	ROE	Current Ratio	Dividend Yield	Earnings per Share
Research Notes					Date	Price

Stock Buying Watchlist

Company				Code	Sector	Index	Market Cap
P/E Ratio	EV/EBITDA	Debt-to-Equity		ROE	Current Ratio	Dividend Yield	Earnings per Share
Research Notes						Date	Price

Company				Code	Sector	Index	Market Cap
P/E Ratio	EV/EBITDA	Debt-to-Equity		ROE	Current Ratio	Dividend Yield	Earnings per Share
Research Notes						Date	Price

Company				Code	Sector	Index	Market Cap
P/E Ratio	EV/EBITDA	Debt-to-Equity		ROE	Current Ratio	Dividend Yield	Earnings per Share
Research Notes						Date	Price

Company				Code	Sector	Index	Market Cap
P/E Ratio	EV/EBITDA	Debt-to-Equity		ROE	Current Ratio	Dividend Yield	Earnings per Share
Research Notes						Date	Price

Stock Buying Watchlist

Company				Code	Sector		Index	Market Cap
P/E Ratio	EV/EBITDA	Debt-to-Equity		ROE	Current Ratio		Dividend Yield	Earnings per Share
Research Notes							Date	Price

Company				Code	Sector		Index	Market Cap
P/E Ratio	EV/EBITDA	Debt-to-Equity		ROE	Current Ratio		Dividend Yield	Earnings per Share
Research Notes							Date	Price

Company				Code	Sector		Index	Market Cap
P/E Ratio	EV/EBITDA	Debt-to-Equity		ROE	Current Ratio		Dividend Yield	Earnings per Share
Research Notes							Date	Price

Company				Code	Sector		Index	Market Cap
P/E Ratio	EV/EBITDA	Debt-to-Equity		ROE	Current Ratio		Dividend Yield	Earnings per Share
Research Notes							Date	Price

Stock Buying Watchlist

Company			Code	Sector	Index	Market Cap
P/E Ratio	EV/EBITDA	Debt-to-Equity	ROE	Current Ratio	Dividend Yield	Earnings per Share
Research Notes					Date	Price

Company			Code	Sector	Index	Market Cap
P/E Ratio	EV/EBITDA	Debt-to-Equity	ROE	Current Ratio	Dividend Yield	Earnings per Share
Research Notes					Date	Price

Company			Code	Sector	Index	Market Cap
P/E Ratio	EV/EBITDA	Debt-to-Equity	ROE	Current Ratio	Dividend Yield	Earnings per Share
Research Notes					Date	Price

Company			Code	Sector	Index	Market Cap
P/E Ratio	EV/EBITDA	Debt-to-Equity	ROE	Current Ratio	Dividend Yield	Earnings per Share
Research Notes					Date	Price

Stock Buying Watchlist

Company				Code	Sector		Index	Market Cap
P/E Ratio	EV/EBITDA		Debt-to-Equity	ROE	Current Ratio		Dividend Yield	Earnings per Share
Research Notes							Date	Price

Company				Code	Sector		Index	Market Cap
P/E Ratio	EV/EBITDA		Debt-to-Equity	ROE	Current Ratio		Dividend Yield	Earnings per Share
Research Notes							Date	Price

Company				Code	Sector		Index	Market Cap
P/E Ratio	EV/EBITDA		Debt-to-Equity	ROE	Current Ratio		Dividend Yield	Earnings per Share
Research Notes							Date	Price

Company				Code	Sector		Index	Market Cap
P/E Ratio	EV/EBITDA		Debt-to-Equity	ROE	Current Ratio		Dividend Yield	Earnings per Share
Research Notes							Date	Price

Stock Buying Watchlist

Company			Code	Sector	Index	Market Cap
P/E Ratio	EV/EBITDA	Debt-to-Equity	ROE	Current Ratio	Dividend Yield	Earnings per Share
Research Notes					Date	Price

Company			Code	Sector	Index	Market Cap
P/E Ratio	EV/EBITDA	Debt-to-Equity	ROE	Current Ratio	Dividend Yield	Earnings per Share
Research Notes					Date	Price

Company			Code	Sector	Index	Market Cap
P/E Ratio	EV/EBITDA	Debt-to-Equity	ROE	Current Ratio	Dividend Yield	Earnings per Share
Research Notes					Date	Price

Company			Code	Sector	Index	Market Cap
P/E Ratio	EV/EBITDA	Debt-to-Equity	ROE	Current Ratio	Dividend Yield	Earnings per Share
Research Notes					Date	Price

Stock Buying Watchlist

Company			Code	Sector	Index	Market Cap
P/E Ratio	EV/EBITDA	Debt-to-Equity	ROE	Current Ratio	Dividend Yield	Earnings per Share
Research Notes					Date	Price

Company			Code	Sector	Index	Market Cap
P/E Ratio	EV/EBITDA	Debt-to-Equity	ROE	Current Ratio	Dividend Yield	Earnings per Share
Research Notes					Date	Price

Company			Code	Sector	Index	Market Cap
P/E Ratio	EV/EBITDA	Debt-to-Equity	ROE	Current Ratio	Dividend Yield	Earnings per Share
Research Notes					Date	Price

Company			Code	Sector	Index	Market Cap
P/E Ratio	EV/EBITDA	Debt-to-Equity	ROE	Current Ratio	Dividend Yield	Earnings per Share
Research Notes					Date	Price

Stock Buying Watchlist

Company			Code	Sector	Index	Market Cap
P/E Ratio	EV/EBITDA	Debt-to-Equity	ROE	Current Ratio	Dividend Yield	Earnings per Share
Research Notes					Date	Price

Company			Code	Sector	Index	Market Cap
P/E Ratio	EV/EBITDA	Debt-to-Equity	ROE	Current Ratio	Dividend Yield	Earnings per Share
Research Notes					Date	Price

Company			Code	Sector	Index	Market Cap
P/E Ratio	EV/EBITDA	Debt-to-Equity	ROE	Current Ratio	Dividend Yield	Earnings per Share
Research Notes					Date	Price

Company			Code	Sector	Index	Market Cap
P/E Ratio	EV/EBITDA	Debt-to-Equity	ROE	Current Ratio	Dividend Yield	Earnings per Share
Research Notes					Date	Price

Stock Buying Watchlist

Company			Code	Sector	Index	Market Cap
P/E Ratio	EV/EBITDA	Debt-to-Equity	ROE	Current Ratio	Dividend Yield	Earnings per Share
Research Notes					Date	Price

Company			Code	Sector	Index	Market Cap
P/E Ratio	EV/EBITDA	Debt-to-Equity	ROE	Current Ratio	Dividend Yield	Earnings per Share
Research Notes					Date	Price

Company			Code	Sector	Index	Market Cap
P/E Ratio	EV/EBITDA	Debt-to-Equity	ROE	Current Ratio	Dividend Yield	Earnings per Share
Research Notes					Date	Price

Company			Code	Sector	Index	Market Cap
P/E Ratio	EV/EBITDA	Debt-to-Equity	ROE	Current Ratio	Dividend Yield	Earnings per Share
Research Notes					Date	Price

Stock Buying Watchlist

Company			Code	Sector	Index	Market Cap
P/E Ratio	EV/EBITDA	Debt-to-Equity	ROE	Current Ratio	Dividend Yield	Earnings per Share
Research Notes					Date	Price

Company			Code	Sector	Index	Market Cap
P/E Ratio	EV/EBITDA	Debt-to-Equity	ROE	Current Ratio	Dividend Yield	Earnings per Share
Research Notes					Date	Price

Company			Code	Sector	Index	Market Cap
P/E Ratio	EV/EBITDA	Debt-to-Equity	ROE	Current Ratio	Dividend Yield	Earnings per Share
Research Notes					Date	Price

Company			Code	Sector	Index	Market Cap
P/E Ratio	EV/EBITDA	Debt-to-Equity	ROE	Current Ratio	Dividend Yield	Earnings per Share
Research Notes					Date	Price

Stock Buying Watchlist

Company				Code	Sector	Index	Market Cap
P/E Ratio	EV/EBITDA	Debt-to-Equity		ROE	Current Ratio	Dividend Yield	Earnings per Share
Research Notes						Date	Price

Company				Code	Sector	Index	Market Cap
P/E Ratio	EV/EBITDA	Debt-to-Equity		ROE	Current Ratio	Dividend Yield	Earnings per Share
Research Notes						Date	Price

Company				Code	Sector	Index	Market Cap
P/E Ratio	EV/EBITDA	Debt-to-Equity		ROE	Current Ratio	Dividend Yield	Earnings per Share
Research Notes						Date	Price

Company				Code	Sector	Index	Market Cap
P/E Ratio	EV/EBITDA	Debt-to-Equity		ROE	Current Ratio	Dividend Yield	Earnings per Share
Research Notes						Date	Price

Stock Buying Watchlist

Company			Code	Sector	Index	Market Cap
P/E Ratio	EV/EBITDA	Debt-to-Equity	ROE	Current Ratio	Dividend Yield	Earnings per Share
Research Notes					Date	Price

Company			Code	Sector	Index	Market Cap
P/E Ratio	EV/EBITDA	Debt-to-Equity	ROE	Current Ratio	Dividend Yield	Earnings per Share
Research Notes					Date	Price

Company			Code	Sector	Index	Market Cap
P/E Ratio	EV/EBITDA	Debt-to-Equity	ROE	Current Ratio	Dividend Yield	Earnings per Share
Research Notes					Date	Price

Company			Code	Sector	Index	Market Cap
P/E Ratio	EV/EBITDA	Debt-to-Equity	ROE	Current Ratio	Dividend Yield	Earnings per Share
Research Notes					Date	Price

Stock Buying Watchlist

Company				Code	Sector	Index	Market Cap
P/E Ratio	EV/EBITDA	Debt-to-Equity		ROE	Current Ratio	Dividend Yield	Earnings per Share
Research Notes						Date	Price

Company				Code	Sector	Index	Market Cap
P/E Ratio	EV/EBITDA	Debt-to-Equity		ROE	Current Ratio	Dividend Yield	Earnings per Share
Research Notes						Date	Price

Company				Code	Sector	Index	Market Cap
P/E Ratio	EV/EBITDA	Debt-to-Equity		ROE	Current Ratio	Dividend Yield	Earnings per Share
Research Notes						Date	Price

Company				Code	Sector	Index	Market Cap
P/E Ratio	EV/EBITDA	Debt-to-Equity		ROE	Current Ratio	Dividend Yield	Earnings per Share
Research Notes						Date	Price

Stock Buying Watchlist

Company				Code	Sector	Index	Market Cap
P/E Ratio	EV/EBITDA	Debt-to-Equity		ROE	Current Ratio	Dividend Yield	Earnings per Share
Research Notes						Date	Price

Company				Code	Sector	Index	Market Cap
P/E Ratio	EV/EBITDA	Debt-to-Equity		ROE	Current Ratio	Dividend Yield	Earnings per Share
Research Notes						Date	Price

Company				Code	Sector	Index	Market Cap
P/E Ratio	EV/EBITDA	Debt-to-Equity		ROE	Current Ratio	Dividend Yield	Earnings per Share
Research Notes						Date	Price

Company				Code	Sector	Index	Market Cap
P/E Ratio	EV/EBITDA	Debt-to-Equity		ROE	Current Ratio	Dividend Yield	Earnings per Share
Research Notes						Date	Price

Designed by SkullPilot Publishing
Copyright © SkullPilot Publishing (2019)

Made in the USA
Monee, IL
12 October 2020